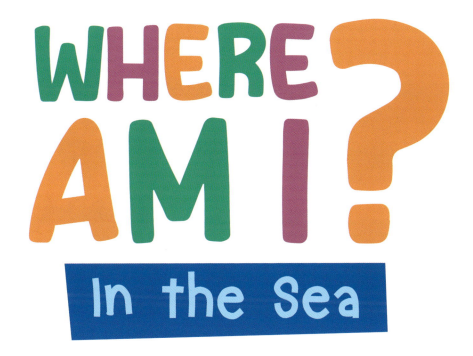

Written by Noah Leatherland

Published in 2025 by Enslow Publishing, LLC
2544 Clinton Street
Buffalo, NY 14224

© 2024 BookLife Publishing Ltd.

Written by:
Noah Leatherland

Edited by:
Rebecca Phillips-Bartlett

Designed by:
Amy Li

Cataloging-in-Publication Data

Names: Leatherland, Noah, 1999-.
Title: In the sea / Noah Leatherland.
Description: Buffalo, NY : Enslow Publishing, 2025. | Series: Where am I? | Includes glossary.
Identifiers: ISBN 9781978541771 (pbk.) | ISBN 9781978541788 (library bound) | ISBN 9781978541795 (ebook)
Subjects: LCSH: Marine animals--Juvenile literature. | Marine animals--Habitation--Juvenile literature. | Marine ecology--Juvenile literature.
Classification: LCC QL122.2 L38 2025 | DDC 591.77--dc23

All rights reserved.

No part of this book may be reproduced in any form without permission in writing from the publisher, except by a reviewer.

Manufactured in the United States of America

CPSIA compliance information: Batch #CW25ENS: For further information contact Enslow Publishing LLC at 1-800-398-2504.

Please visit our website, www.enslowpublishing.com. For a free color catalog of all our high-quality books, call toll free 1-800-398-2504 or fax 1-877-980-4454.

Find us on

PHOTO CREDITS All images are courtesy of Shutterstock.com, unless otherwise specified. With thanks to Getty Images, Thinkstock Photo and iStockphoto.
Recurring – Net Vector, Natalllenka.m, Water Shine. Cover – ankomando, MaeManee, MWFP84, natchapohn, StockSmartStart, Thierry Eidenweil. 2–3 – RayK Photos. 4–5 – Dudarev Mikhail, Pete Niesen. 6–7 – Artur_Sarkisyan, StockSmartStart. 8–9 – Vladimir Wrangel, blue-sea.cz, GrapeRoni. 10–11 – Dmitry Rukhlenko, natchapohn. 12–13 – Ekkapan Poddamrong, Tappasan Phurisamrit, StockSmartStart. 14–15 – FtLaud, ankomando. 16–17 – nickeverett1981, Innerspace Images, StockSmartStart. 18–19 – Craig Lambert Photography, Maquiladora. 20–21 – Andrea Izzotti, Gerald Robert Fischer. 22–23 – Aastels, Javier Hdez Photography.

CONTENTS

PAGE 4	Where Am I?
PAGE 6	Octopus
PAGE 8	Stonefish
PAGE 10	Leafy Sea Dragon
PAGE 12	Decorator Crab
PAGE 14	Flounder
PAGE 16	Pygmy Seahorse
PAGE 18	Humpback Whale
PAGE 20	Stargazer Fish
PAGE 22	Hiding in the Habitat
PAGE 24	Glossary and Index

Words that look like this can be found in the glossary on page 24.

WHERE AM I?

The sea is huge! More than half of Earth is covered by the ocean. These huge habitats are home to thousands of different creatures of all shapes and sizes.

A habitat is where an animal lives and has everything they need to survive.

Danger can come from all directions in an underwater habitat. Some sea creatures are excellent hunters and powerful <u>predators</u>. Other sea creatures have to be super sneaky to hide from them.

OCTOPUS

I am an octopus. I have no bones in my body. This is very useful when I am looking for somewhere to hide. My soft body lets me tuck myself away to hide in small gaps and tight spaces.

I also have excellent <u>camouflage</u>. I can change the color and <u>texture</u> of my skin to match my surroundings. This lets me hide from my predators and my <u>prey</u>.

STONEFISH

I am a stonefish. I can be found living near <u>coral reefs</u> and rocks. I have <u>adapted</u> to look like the rocks in my habitat. This makes me very hard to spot!

I have a way of protecting myself just in case anything gets too close. I have pointy parts along my body called spines. If something touches these spines, they get a nasty sting!

Can you spot me?

LEAFY SEA DRAGON

I am a leafy sea dragon. Some sea creatures have body parts that look like things in their habitat. I have appendages that look just like pieces of seaweed. This helps me camouflage myself.

DECORATOR CRAB

I am a decorator crab. I cannot change color or squeeze into gaps. Instead, I find things in my habitat and stick them onto my body to help me camouflage.

I have tiny hooked hairs on my body that I can stick things onto. I often stick tiny living things onto myself, such as sea sponges or seaweed.

Where am I?

FLOUNDER

I am a flounder. I live at the bottom of the sea. I am very flat so that I can lie along the ocean floor. Sometimes I bury myself in the sand to hide.

Where am I hiding?

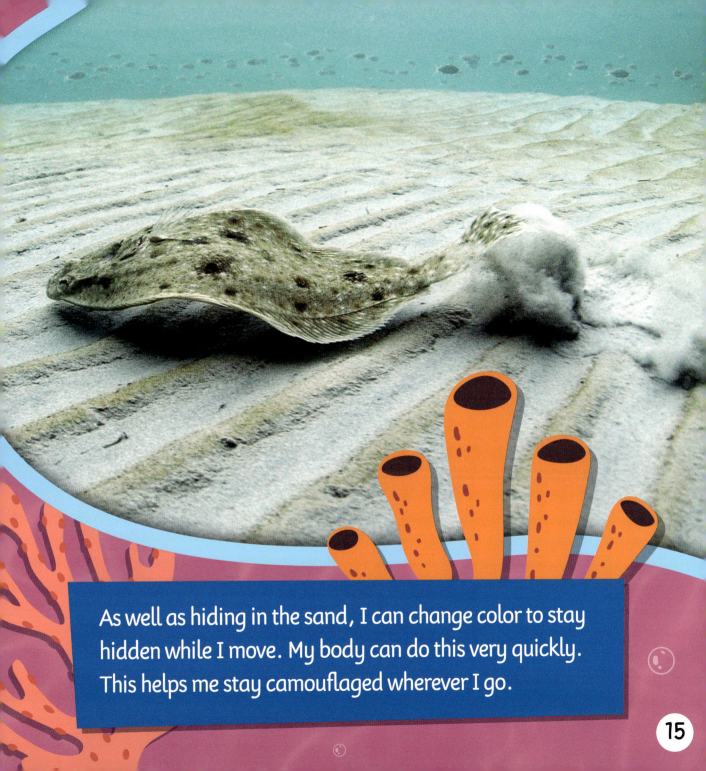

As well as hiding in the sand, I can change color to stay hidden while I move. My body can do this very quickly. This helps me stay camouflaged wherever I go.

PYGMY SEAHORSE

I am a pygmy seahorse. I am the smallest kind of seahorse in the world! I am usually between 0.4 and 0.8 inch (1 and 2 cm) long. However, being so small is not the only thing that makes me hard to spot.

I can change color to match my <u>environment</u>. Pygmy seahorses like me can be found in coral reefs. Coral reefs give us plenty of places to hide and different colors to blend in with.

HUMPBACK WHALE

I am a humpback whale. I am very big, but I can still hide by using the colors of my skin as camouflage. I have dark patches on my back and light patches underneath.

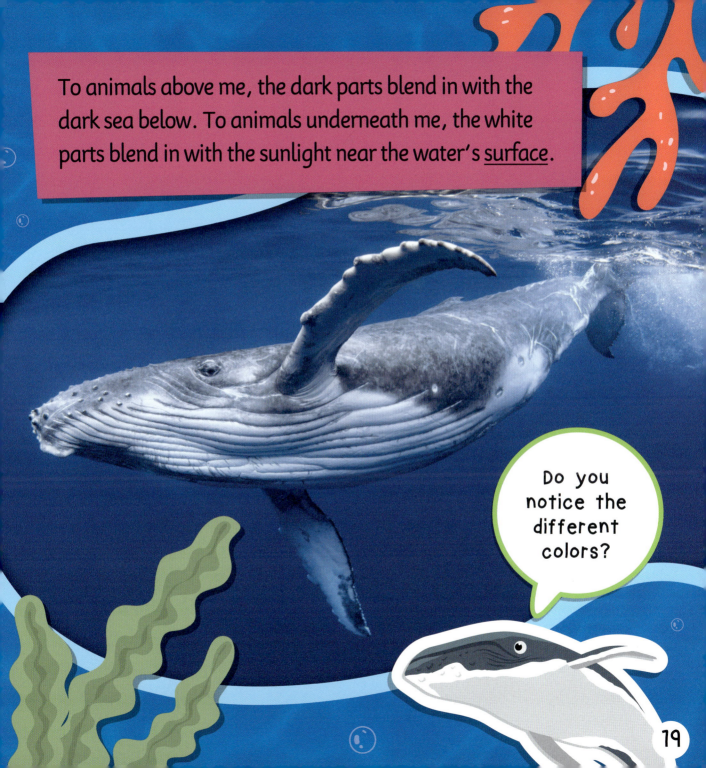

STARGAZER FISH

I am a stargazer fish. My eyes and mouth face upward. The strange shape of my face helps me hide in my habitat. I bury myself in the sand at the bottom of the sea.

With my body under the sand, my eyes and mouth face upward to the water above. I wait until I spot my prey swimming close to me. Then I quickly gobble them up!

Can you spot me?

HIDING IN THE HABITAT

Using camouflage and finding places to hide is very important for wild animals. Staying out of sight helps some animals hide from predators. It also helps predators sneak up on their prey.

A CLOWNFISH HIDING IN AN ANEMONE

A CROCODILEFISH BLENDING IN WITH THE ROCKS

Animals can be found hiding away and using camouflage in environments all over the world. Or maybe they can't be found. It depends how good they are at hiding!

GLOSSARY

ADAPTED changed over time to suit the environment

APPENDAGES body parts that grow from the main body

CAMOUFLAGE the ability to blend in with the surroundings

CORAL REEFS underwater habitats made up of the bodies of tiny animals

ENVIRONMENT the surroundings in which an animal or plant lives or spends time

PREDATORS animals that hunt other animals for food

PREY animals that are hunted by other animals for food

SURFACE the top layer of a body of water

TEXTURE the feel or look of something

INDEX

BONES 6

CORAL REEFS 8, 17

EYES 20–21

HAIRS 13

ROCKS 8, 23

SAND 14–15, 20–21

SEAWEED 10–11, 13

SKIN 7, 18

SPINES 9